Will You Remember?

By Chanda Minor Brigance

One Printers Way
Altona, MB R0G 0B0
Canada

www.friesenpress.com

Copyright © 2022 by Chanda Minor Brigance
First Edition — 2022
Mariya Stoyanova
Illustrator

BEAM OF LIGHT, LLC
Chanda Minor Brigance
"CHAN Is A Caregiver™"
Author & Caregiving Advocate
Follow me on Facebook
www.chandaminorbrigance.com
caringis4me@gmail.com

All rights reserved.

No part of this publication may be reproduced in any form, or by any means, electronic or mechanical, including photocopying, recording, or any information browsing, storage, or retrieval system, without permission in writing from

FriesenPress.

ISBN
978-1-03-913447-8 (Hardcover)
978-1-03-913446-1 (Paperback)
978-1-03-913448-5 (eBook)

1. JUVENILE NONFICTION, HEALTH & DAILY LIVING, DISEASES, ILLNESSES & INJURIES

Distributed to the trade by The Ingram Book Company

Will You Remember?

From the

"CHAN IS A CAREGIVER™"

collection

*Grandchildren are the crown of the aged;
and parents are the pride of their children.*

Proverbs 17:6 NIV

To my sweet and dear MomMom
whom I will always remember

Hello!

I'm

CHAN

the caregiver.

I want to tell you how *I remember* being the loving caregiver for my MomMom.

A caregiver is someone who gives care to another person who needs help taking care of themselves.

My MomMom was my sweet grandma. She was also my friend.

I remember having lots of fun times and doing lots of fun things with my MomMom.

I remember my MomMom clapping her hands to the beat of my marching while I twirled my baton.

I remember my MomMom waving flags and cheering for me during my cheerleading events.

Cheerleading was exciting and so much fun.

I remember jumping as high as the sky!

I remember my MomMom waking up early in the morning and helping me get ready for school.

My MomMom would wave goodbye to me while saying, "Have a good day at school."

Suddenly, one day, out of nowhere, my MomMom seemed very different. My MomMom was not herself.

I soon realized my MomMom no longer remembered me or any of the fun times we had together.

This made me feel very sad and hurt.

I remember crying in my bedroom. I thought I had done something wrong that had hurt my MomMom.

I felt I had lost my best friend and my grandma.
I felt all alone.

I later learned that I had done nothing wrong.

My MomMom had Alzheimer's disease.

Alzheimer's disease is a sickness that often causes a person to become confused and forgetful.

This meant my MomMom would need a loving caregiver.

My MomMom would need me . . .

CHAN

the caregiver.

Caregiving for my MomMom meant I would help her.

I remember caring for my MomMom by helping her remember to take her bubble bath.

My MomMom enjoyed bubble baths with lots and lots of fun bubbles!

I also cared for my MomMom by making sure she had *YUMMY* foods to eat.

I remember caring for my MomMom by helping her find her favorite purple dress.

I remember caring for my MomMom by holding her hand as she walked on the sidewalk so she would not fall.

My MomMom and I would often have fun daydreaming.

I remember daydreaming about my MomMom and I going on long and exciting car rides together on warm sunny days.

I pictured my MomMom throwing her arms into the air and letting the cool wind blow through her fingertips!

Although my MomMom had Alzheimer's disease, she still seemed happy on some days.

But as time went by, the fun times ended. Now, sweet memories are all I have left of my MomMom.

I will always love you,

I will always remember you,

MomMom

"Have you lost someone close to you?

Will you remember all the fun times you had together?"

Will you remember?

This inspiring true story is dedicated to all caregivers who give care and love to someone special!

You can care for someone in need by:
- Reading a fun book to them
- Helping them with crafts
- Playing music for them

or maybe

- Planting a beautiful garden with them

What will you do?

THE END

Printed in the USA
CPSIA information can be obtained
at www.ICGtesting.com
LVHW060849100124
768548LV00019B/804